CONGRESSIONAL INTERVENTION IN REGARD TO SLAVERY IN THE TERRITORIES.

LETTER

OF

LAWRENCE O'B. BRANCH

TO

HIS CONSTITUENTS.

MAY 15, 1860.

WASHINGTON:
PRINTED AT THE CONGRESSIONAL GLOBE OFFICE.
1860.

LETTER.

The systematic agitation of the slavery question by the northern people with a view to retard the growth and curtail the political power of the southern states, may be said to have commenced about thirty years ago.

The avowed object then was the abolition of slavery in the District of Columbia, in the forts, arsenals, and dockyards belonging to the government, and in Florida, which was the only organized Territory of the Union. The means of agitation adopted was to flood Congress with immense numbers of petitions signed by men, women, and children, praying for those objects.

No fear was entertained by the South of any action by Congress favorable to the object of the petitioners, for there were not at that time twenty avowed Abolitionists in both its branches; but so averse were our representatives to the introduction of the subject into Congress, on any pretext or for any purpose, that they adopted the very extreme policy of objecting to even the reception of the petitions.

If in this they erred at all, it was from excess of anxiety to keep the subject out of Congress.

After a few years this agitation assumed a new and more practical form. The new system of attack was embodied in the Wilmot proviso, by which it was proposed to exclude slavery from all the Territories by act of Congress. So rapid had been the growth of abolitionism that the Congress which sat in 1848 was probably in favor of the proviso, and, under a subterfuge, it was ingrafted on the Oregon bill. The South resisted it not only on grounds of justice and equality, but as a breach of the Constitution. We insisted that every community should be permitted to regulate its own domestic affairs at such time and in such way as the Constitution allows, and that any interference by Congress was inexpedient and unjust, if not unconstitutional.

The "Clayton compromise" which was offered in the same year, was simply a proposition that Congress should take no cognizance of the subject, leaving it to the local law, under the adjudication of the courts. The whole South, including Mr. Calhoun, advocated and voted for it, except eight Whig members of the House of Representatives and two members of the Senate.

I lay no stress on the fact that General Cass was nominated and voted for by the South, after he wrote the "Nicholson letter," for there was a difference of opinion at the time as to what the letter meant on one point. All agreed, however, that it meant total non-interference by Congress, and so well did that suit the views of the South that we were willing to forgive his equivocal language about squatter sovereignty.

Then came the "compromise measures" of 1850. By them we gave up the slave trade in the District of Columbia; the admission of California, (the original of squatter sovereignty,) and enough of Texas to make a State. And what did we get in return for these large concessions? A fugitive slave law, no better than that we already had, because the northern States will not allow either to be executed within their limits; a stipulation that Utah and New Mexico should "be admitted into the Union with or without slavery, as their constitutions should prescribe;" and, what we valued most of all, an understanding that thereafter non-intervention by Congress should be the established policy of the government. So eager were we to keep the slavery question out of Congress, that we seem to have thought scarcely any price too great to pay for it.

Next in order came the Kansas and Nebraska act of 1854.

In 1850 we had obtained non-interference by Congress in Utah and New Mexico, and a promise of the same as to future Territories. We had paid a high price in advance, and in 1854 it was to be determined whether the bargain would be adhered to. Non-intervention by Congress, a total and final exclusion of the slavery question from Congress, were everywhere proclaimed as our watchwords. We carried Congress; we carried States; we elected the President on it. After twenty years of hard struggle, through all of which we kept this one point constantly and steadily in view, we triumphed and established it as the fixed policy of the government that thereafter Congress should not discuss slavery, nor agitate it, nor legislate about it, except to carry out the express provisions of the Constitution.

That in this long and murderous warfare upon her dearest rights, the South may have committed some errors in matters of policy, is not improbable. She may have accepted issues she ought not to have accepted; she may even have pushed sound principles to excess sometimes; but the tenacity with which she has clung to the one idea of excluding the slavery question from Congress is worthy of all commendation, and has mainly contributed to her ultimate success.

In view of the fact that within the last ten years a fugitive slave law has been passed as stringent in its provisions as we asked for—the odious Missouri compromise has been repealed—the Dred Scott decision has been rendered—and non-intervention by Congress has been established—a distinguished Senator from Georgia [Mr. TOOMBS] could truly declare in the Senate, a short time ago, that at no time in its history had the federal government more faithfully discharged its duty to the South than within the last ten years. The evils under which we suffer are not caused by the failure of Congress to do its duty, but by the nullification of its laws by northern States, and the treasonable conduct of their citizens.

Having thus briefly brought under notice the prominent points in the history of the slavery agitation, with a view to remind you that non-interference by Congress is what the South has heretofore contended for; I am prepared to enter upon the discussion of a new doctrine, recently made prominent, which promises no present advantage to the South, and which may ultimately deprive its citizens of all participation in the common Territories of the Union. I allude to the doctrine of CONGRESSIONAL PROTECTION TO SLAVERY IN THE TERRITORIES. The disruption of the Democratic Convention at Charleston is its first fruit; but fortunately the delegates assembled there were not entirely bereft of their senses, and, by adjourning over to Richmond and Baltimore, they have placed it in the power of the Democratic people to interpose and save us from ruin.

Will you insist on having that doctrine incorporated into the platform of the Democratic party, as the sole condition on which you will act with it in the approaching contest with the Republican party?

Or are you willing to beat the Republican party on the same terms we have heretofore beaten them on, rather than not beat them at all?

That is the question you are to decide between this and the 18th of June, when the Convention will reassemble in Baltimore, and it is fairly stated, for I have not seen an individual who believes that either fragment of the Democratic party can defeat them single-handed, and many are of opinion that both combined cannot accomplish the good work.

At a time so full of perils as the present, I would feel disinclined to ask for the adoption of any new tenet, even if it promised additional security to the South. But, in this new doctrine, I see, under the insidious garb of protection, nothing but hidden dangers, and a surrender, even before the adversary has demanded it, of all the fruits of twenty years of successful struggle with Freesoilism and Abolitionism. The whole doctrine is embodied in three propositions, which I will state:

I. The citizens of the slaveholding States have a right to remove with their slaves into the Territories of the Union, and the territorial legislatures cannot abolish slavery so as to deprive them of their property.

II. It is the duty of the territorial legislatures to pass all laws necessary for the protection of the slave owner in the full and convenient enjoyment of his property.

III. If the territorial legislatures pass laws to injure him, or fail to pass laws to protect him, it is the duty of Congress to pass all such laws for the Territories so failing as are necessary to enable the slave owner to use and enjoy his property conveniently and advantageously.

In the first proposition I entirely concur. Whatever right of property in a personal chattel I may have acquired under the constitution and laws of a State of the Union will accompany me into any of the Territories to which I may carry it; and until the inhabitants of the Territory can, with the consent of Congress and pursuant to the principles and provisions of the Constitution, exercise sovereign powers, there is no authority there competent to divest me of my right of property. The Constitution of the United States does not create the right by which I hold my slave in a Territory, but simply protects against violation a right acquired under the constitution and laws of a State.

As far back as in 1848 I had occasion to publish my opinion on what has been called "squatter sovereignty." I then said:

"It would be easy enough to show that a mere temporary government, owing its existence and all its powers to an act of Congress, and that of doubtful constitutionality, organized because there are not people enough to sustain a government for themselves, cannot assume to fix and alter the fundamental institutions of society, not only for themselves but for the much larger number who are expected and encouraged by the general government to come after them; excluding whom and what they please from a vast extent of common territory, and admitting only whom and what they may choose."

And again, in a speech which I delived in the House of Representatives, in December, 1856, I said:

"That such a body [a territorial legislature] possesses power to annul rights of property acquired and held under the common law and constitutions of fifteen States of the Union, appears to me a proposition too monstrous to be entertained for a moment in a nation not prepared to revert to barbarism and anarchy.

"For my part, I do not think it [the establishment of what shall be, or what shall not be, property] a rightful subject of legislation; and hence I do not think the Kansas and Nebraska act, or the Constitution, confers any such power on the legislature, and I am satisfied the Supreme Court will so decide, if the question should ever arise.

"Will the Democratic party, especially will the southern portion of it, fall into the snare laid for it by the Fillmore men of the South and the Black Republicans of the North? Shall we quarrel over the bone of contention cast into our midst by the honorable gentleman from Kentucky, [Mr. Humphrey Marshal?] Whatever others may do, I will not. I do not believe the Kansas-Nebraska bill empowers the territorial legislature to exclude the slaveholder with his property; but I am willing for that question to take the course of other constitutional questions, and be decided by the courts, as the bill intended it should be decided."

The opinions I then expressed remain unchanged, and the subsequent decision of the Supreme Court in the Dred Scott case has verified my prediction as to what its decision would be. If there is a doubt as to what was decided in that case, the court is the proper tribunal to interpret its own decisions; and, as a politician, I want no better platform to stand upon on a judicial question than a decision of the Supreme Court of the United States. By contemporaneous pledges, and by every consideration of sound principle, the party to which I am attached stands bound to respect differences of opinion—and to tolerate them, too—in all those who, in good faith, will stand to and abide by the decisions of the Supreme Court on this question of squatter sovereignty.

This question was discussed when the Kansas and Nebraska bill was pending in 1854. Some said the people of a Territory had a right to legislate against slavery before their admission into the Union; others said that, under the Constitution, they could not possess or exercise any such right. All agreed that the extent of their right, under the Constitution, was a judicial question, to be decided by the Supreme Court; and all agreed to abide by the decision of the court when it should be made. And, in order that the courts might be open for the decision of the question, the ninth section of the bill provided that appeals might be taken from the territorial courts to the Supreme Court of the United States, in all cases "involving title to slaves," "without regard to the value of the matter, property, or title in controversy," showing clearly that the bill contemplated the settlement of this question by the courts, and not by Congress. Otherwise, a resident in a Territory would not have been allowed an appeal to the Supreme Court in a case in which such appeal is not allowed to the citizen of a State.

In 1856 the question existed in precisely the same dimensions, and having the same bearings as at present. We did not make it a test then; least of all, did we say that we could not, without a sacrifice of principle, act with those who differed from us in opinion as to how the Court would probably decide the question? If we had done so, Mr. Frémont would now be President instead of Mr. Buchanan. What reason can be assigned for making it a test now, which was not equally cogent in 1856? None whatever.

To the second proposition I also give my assent.

To protect persons and property within the limits of its jurisdiction is the sole purpose for which a legislature is instituted, and, when it fails to discharge that duty, it is recreant to its trust, and should meet the condemnation of every honest citizen. Amongst a people virtuous enough for self-government, such a dereliction from duty as a failure to pass laws for the protection of the citizen in the enjoyment of property declared to be his by the highest courts of the land, will meet the condemnation it deserves, and hurl the faithless legislators from the places they unworthily fill. The passage of laws hostile to property would make good men pray for despotism, to save them from ruthless anarchy.

But, unfortunately, we know that the Abolitionist scruples at no outrage, and glories in that of which other men would be ashamed. He is restrained by no constitutional inhibitions, and is ever anxious to signalize his zeal by outrage and fraud. Suppose they shall attempt to perpetrate the outrage here alluded to, as they have actually done in Kansas and Nebraska, and as I have no doubt they will do wherever they have the majority—what remedy have we?

This brings me to the third and main proposition. If they attempt to exclude us, or to deprive us of our property, or to harass us by actual legislation, the remedy is clear, and will be efficient so long as the federal judiciary is kept pure. Any aggrieved citizen can contest the constitutionality of the law, and when the court has decided in his favor, as the Dred Scott decision assures us it will decide, the President is bound to see its decree obeyed and for that purpose can use the whole military and naval resources of the country. If the executive arm is not sufficiently strong for the purpose under existing laws, it is the duty of Congress to pass such additional laws as may be necessary to enable the President to discharge efficiently this his first and highest duty under the Constitution. This is as much protection as any of us have or can have against bad laws under a constitutional government, and more than we could have under any other; and if it is not perfect it is because human institutions cannot entirely eradicate human vices, nor bridle the selfish and malevolent passions of individuals.

The remedy through the courts would be effective to prevent a territorial legislature from assailing the slave owner by hostile legislation. But what slave owner would leave the fertile lands, and the friendly laws and congenial society of our southern States, to settle in the midst of Abolitionists, where he knew that nothing less than chains would secure his slave from running away or being stolen, and where constantly harassed with law suits and criminal prosecutions, he could only be maintained in the possession of his property by the army and navy of the United States?

In a legal sense his rights and remedies might be complete and perfect. He might repose the fullest confidence in the President and federal judiciary, who have shown themselves obedient to their oaths and true to duty even in the worst hot-beds of abolitionism. But I incline to think that no slave owner will ever carry his property to a Territory in which a majority of the inhabitants are known to be Abolitionists. In such a community even the most judicious and friendly laws would not be administered in his favor by abolition judges and juries, whether the laws emanated from Congress or from the local authorities, and the adventurous or confiding slave owner who should escape highway robbery at the hands of the legislature, would probably find himself in a den of thieves when he reached the jury-box. Hence, I announced no political theory but a simple patent fact when I said, in 1856, that "if a majority of the legislature are opposed to slavery there are a multitude of ways in which the slaveholder may be harassed and kept out by hostile legislation, and by a failure to provide remedies for the protection of his rights. Practically the institution can only be introduced and sustained where the majority are willing to tolerate it."

Suppose, however, that instead of legislating affirmatively for the annoyance and injury of the slaveholder, a different system of tactics should be adopted, and the majority should refuse to legislate at all about him or his property; should refuse to pass laws for the punishment of a person who harbors a runaway, or who sells liquor to a slave, or who trades with him for stolen goods, or who inflicts on him an injury without the consent of the owner. We all know there are a multitude of such legal provisions in every slaveholding community, without which there could be no control over the slave population—no discipline—and they would be a nuisance and a curse.

If the legislature should refuse to throw around us these guards, and should leave us a prey to evildoers, what is to be done? Many of these might be held, at least, under the system of jurisprudence prevailing in the southern States, to be offenses at common law—that great body of *lex non scripta* on which every community must rely, to a great extent, for the preservation of order—and might be punished wherever that law is recognized. But it must not be forgotten that the common law can only have force by the express adoption or tacit sufferance of the law-making power.

The advocates of the doctrine I am discussing say that if the legislatures fail to give suitable and adequate protection, Congress must pass what I will for brevity call "slave codes" for the Territories; that is, must take upon itself the local legislation for them, at least to that extent.

I cannot give my assent to this proposition; and in discussing it, I propose to confine myself to considerations of expediency, without going at all into the much higher and broader question of the constitutional power of Congress in and over the Territories. My present object is not to seek the boundaries of power, but to show that if Congress has the right to do this thing, it ought not to be exercised; and above all, that the representatives of the southern States ought not to ask for nor consent to it.

Four fifths of the time of Congress, even now, is taken up with questions connected with the Territories and their inhabitants. From the conflicting claims of two squatters to a quarter section of land to the most absurd pretensions to sovereignty over whole empires, of which not one foot is theirs, every local dispute and every vast scheme of plunder seeks admittance into Congress to choke up the channels of legislation, and to infuse gall and bitterness into the councils of the great Republic. If the most important national interests are neglected—if commerce and all its attendant interests are left to the guardianship of subordinates in the Treasury Department—if the relations of the Confederacy with the other powers of the earth are left exclusively to the President and Senate—if sixty millions of dollars per annum are levied on the people under a system of revenue dictated by a combination of interested parties, the details and principles of which are almost utterly unknown to the peoples' representatives—if these sixty millions are annually appropriated by Congress without examination as to the objects of the expenditure, without discussion as to their necessity or propriety, and often without the appropriation bills being even read to or by the members of the House of Representatives—if all these things are habitually and notoriously done, and the great interests of the States and their citizens are shamefully neglected—it is because the Territories have taken possession of Congress, and consume the time and absorb the faculties of the peoples' representatives. If we stand now on the brink of the precipice, and look down into the yawning gulf of dissolution and civil war, it was opened by the Territories, which have arrayed man against man, State against State, and section against section, and where were trained the bandits and outlaws who are the willing and ready instruments of murder and treason.

Under our nursing care the Territories have destroyed the peace of the family by their turbulent conduct, and are now threatening its very existence. Shall we give them more of the time of Congress, and multiply the salient points at which they may assail the peace and quiet of the country by taking upon ourselves their petty criminal and police regulations? For myself, I answer, no! and I believe the great body of the people—at least of the old thirteen States that won our liberties and established our Union—will answer, emphatically, no!

But I have to this proposition still greater objections founded on principle.

For long the Democratic party controlled all the departments of government, and the South, constituting more than half of it, controlled the Democratic party. Under that state of affairs, as I have already shown, the most sensitive and jealous southern statesmen feared to trust to Congress the control of slavery in the Territories. They denied its right to take cognizance of the subject, and resisted every attempt to invoke the action of that body. The Clayton compromise of 1848, which received the ardent support of Mr. Calhoun, owed all its popularity in the South to the fact that it provided for removing the subject from Congress and leaving it to the judiciary and local authorities. The debates on the Kansas and Nebraska bill are graven on the memory of all who are in the habit of reading the political history of the country. We made that bill a test of fidelity to southern rights to the utter overthrow of the northern Democracy, who stood bravely by us, and, with three exceptions, were driven from their seats for the votes they gave on it. That bill never could have been passed, and the

South knows it, but for the desire of patriotic men in both sections to remove the question from Congress, and the belief that the bill would accomplish it.

This great distrust of Congress on the part of the South, I repeat, was exhibited when Congress was comparatively favorable to us and our rights. Now, the state of affairs is changed. One branch of Congress is already under the control of the Republicans, and that party is running us to the throat-latch for the President and Senate. At a time thus inauspicious those who are supposed to be more sensitive than their brothers as to southern rights, come forward and demand congressional intervention.

Non-intervention was the principle of the Kansas and Nebraska bill. As I declared in 1856, before this new issue was raised, it was

"The great, main feature of the bill, infinitely transcending in importance any of the minor questions that can be raised under it." "Under the full and fair operation of which, the question of slavery can no more get into Congress to furnish fuel for the fires of agitation and make the main element in elections, and under which we and our institutions would cease to be a football in the political arena."

I aver that these were the sentiments then entertained by the great bulk of southern men, both in and out of Congress. I will not recall them. Least of all will I go upon the very battle-field on which we fought, and on which, as history records, we of the South gained a glorious victory, and deny the flag under which I did battle.

The Abolitionist is not moved so much by a desire to benefit the negro, as by jealousy and hatred of the owner. He would not be so much pleased at an opportunity to knock the shackles from the slave, as he would be to get it into the power of himself and his associates to harass and annoy the owner. Hence the power to pass a Wilmot proviso, and exclude slaveholders from a Territory, would be less prized by that party than the power to make the domestic and police regulations of the institution. In their most frenzied moments they have never demanded congressional action except to forbid the slaveholder from going to the Territories. They have claimed no right to interfere between him and his slave with a view to regulate their rights and duties to each other. This new doctrine, on the contrary, opens the door of the temple, invites an abolition Congress to the very hearthstone of the slaveholder's domestic circle, and allows it to strike its deadly blows at him in his daily and hourly walks. The nature and extent of rewards and punishments—the amount of labor that may be exacted on one side, and the extent of indulgencies that may be claimed on the other—even the plantation police and discipline—might all be drawn into the vortex of congressional control. A code of rules and regulations on these subjects, prepared by a committee of the indorsers of the Helper book, and submitted to the philosophic mind of the author of the "irrepressible conflict" doctrine, might not be as bloody as the laws of Draco; but, under it, if the slave did not run away from the master, the master would soon run away from the slave.

The advocates of the doctrine, however, contend that the power of Congress does not extend to injuring, but only to protecting slavery. They may be right. I have already said I am not discussing this as a question of power. But some very honest persons will not be able to understand how the existence of a power, under the Constitution, can be made to depend on whether Congress proposes to exercise it for us or against us; and it will be dangerous for us to inculcate the idea that Congress is to exercise any power at all over the subject. But, admitting the restriction on the power as contended for, who is to determine whether any proposed measure will operate as an injury or as a protection? Congress, of course; and we all know that a law which one person or one party considers very salutary is often thought by another person or another party to be ruinous, dangerous, or even revolutionary. The will of the majority will prevail; and, after we have conceded to Congress the right to legislate on the subject, we will find it difficult to arrest legislation when it shall become disagreeable to us. When the allegation is made that a Territory has failed to provide adequate and appropriate protection to slave property, and a bill is introduced into Congress to correct the defects of the local legislation, who is to decide whether the local legislation is adequate and appropriate? Of course, the majority; and that majority is certainly northern and anti-slavery, and may be abolition. What do you suppose a Republican House of Representatives would decide to be adequate and appropriate protection to slave property? Just none at all. We might differ from them; but we are a minority, and cannot pass, nor prevent the passage of a law. So that the least evil we could expect would be the rejection of our bill.

But our enemies might not let us off so easily. Instead of rejecting the bill, they might proceed to amend it so as to make it conform to their notions of the rights of, and the relations that ought to exist between, the white man and his slave; and, having done so, pass it into a law, against our votes. New Mexico, with a resolute integrity and regard for her duties and obligations, which might well be imitated by older citizens of the Republic, has passed a law to protect slave property within her limits. I have read the law, and it is judicious and stringent; but it did not suit the views of the Republicans in the House of Representatives. They did not think the protection it afforded judicious and proper and suitable. It was not in conformity with the moral and economical teachings of the Helper book; they therefore introduced and passed through the House last week a bill disapproving and annulling the law passed by the legislature of New Mexico. Kansas and Nebraska have passed laws against the slaveholder. The same committee that reported the bill to repeal the law of New Mexico have thus far refused, and will continue to refuse, to report a bill to annul the laws of Kansas and Nebraska. That is the kind of protection we may expect from Congress.

No one who has observed the utter disregard of official oaths and obligations, and constitutional restrictions, which has characterized the Abolition party, will doubt that all these things, and more besides, will be done if they have the power. What redress have we? Some say we would dissolve the Union. I think it would be better not to tear away the barrier of the Kansas and Nebraska act which we labored so hard to erect. Behind that we can stand safely. We have not the strength to pass a bill through Congress; all we can do is, by giving up the principle, to throw open the flood-gates and let in abolitionism. I cannot conceive a form in which congressional interference with slavery would be more menacing to the South. The Wilmot proviso would not have brought upon us evils so serious as may, and probably will, flow from this insidious doctrine. The protection we will get from Congress will be such as the wolf gives to the lamb, when admitted into the fold; and when abolitionism has fastened its fangs upon us, in vain will we cry that we called it in to protect, and not to destroy us.

I now invite your attention to the sixth section of the Kansas-Nebraska act, in these words:

"The legislative power of the Territory shall extend to all rightful subjects of legislation consistent with the Constitution of the United States and the provisions of this act."

Is the providing a slave code—that is, laws whereby the owner shall be secured in the convenient enjoyment of his property in his slave—a "rightful subject of legislation?" Of course it is. The very terms of the proposition assume that, in failing to pass such laws, the legislature fails in its duty. The interposition of Congress is only to be asked for when the legislature has failed to discharge its duty in that respect. It being a rightful subject of legislation, full and absolute authority over it was conferred by that act on the territorial legislatures. All preceding acts organizing territorial governments had contained a clause in these words:

"All laws passed by the legislative assembly shall be submitted to the Congress of the United States, and if disapproved, shall be null and of no effect."

This was omitted in the case of Kansas and Nebraska, and the omission of it inaugurated the great principle of non-intervention. This is the distinctive feature, and the only distinctive feature, of that renowned act, for in no other respect does it differ from preceding acts organizing territorial governments.

I put the question distinctly, Would not a resumption by Congress of the right to repeal, alter, or modify the laws of Kansas or Nebraska, be a flat repeal of the sixth section of the act?

Of course, I will not deny the right of Congress to repeal the Kansas-Nebraska act, or any other federal law; but is it expedient to repeal it? Do the southern people wish it repealed? That act has been the battle-cry in every political fight for five years. Our section passed the bill, and those northern Democrats who voted for it were signally rebuked by their constituents. Its unpopularity at the North made the House of Representatives of the Thirty-fourth Congress Republican; its popularity at the South made the South almost a unit in favor of the Democratic party. The last presidential election turned entirely on the same issue. We, the friends of the law, after a struggle unparalleled in the political history of the country, carried the election by a bare majority. Remember how hard we struggled for three years to pass that bill and get it sanctioned by the people. Remember how many northern Democrats fell in the fight. Do not forget that through its popularity we have been enabled to break down the Opposition in every southern State except Maryland. Then answer—Do you wish to repeal it?

If you do, go into sackcloth and ashes for the wrong you inflicted in passing it. Mourn over the gallant northern Democrats destroyed in the unjust fight into which you inveigled them. Make atonement for having defeated Frémont. Return what you have gained in false pretenses. Make restitution of the States you have won from the Opposition. Go tell the people you have deceived them, or that you are not willing to stand by your plighted faith.

Those who choose may do so—I will not. I intend to stand by the Kansas-Nebraska bill in all its parts, in spirit and in letter, and to insist on total, absolute non-intervention by Congress. I will neither make nor join in making any demand which is contradictory of those we have heretofore made, and which we insisted on as tests of fidelity to southern rights. I will never aid to place the South at the mercy of abolitionism, as, in my judgment, this new doctrine would place it.

It may be asked if we are without any remedy for our admitted right to have protection for person and property in the Territories? I answer, no. We are entitled to protection from the local legislature, and if it fails to discharge this high duty, it gives the clearest proof that its constituents are unfit for self-government. In such case, I would withdraw from them the privilege of electing the members of the legislature, and vest the appointment in the President and Senate. That is the remedy I proposed in the case of Utah. It is sound in principle and sanctioned by precedent, and I would apply it to every Territory which proves itself to be unfit for self-government.

What practical advantage is to result from this issue, in whatever manner it may be decided? In what Territory can the question of protection arise? Not in Kansas, for the people of that Territory are already knocking at the door of the Union and will in all probability, whether rightfully or wrongfully, be admitted during this Congress. Whether they are admitted or not, it can have no practical bearing there, because the legislature has attempted to assail the slaveholder by positive legislation, and his remedy is complete in the courts. Not in Nebraska, nor in Oregon, nor in Washington; for there never has been a slave in either of those Territories, and no person believes there ever will be. Not in New Mexico, for the legislature there has already passed a law to protect slave property, if any should ever be taken there. Perhaps the second practical fruit of the doctrine will be the annulment of this law of New Mexico; the first fruit being the destruction of the Democratic party. It certainly would be, if the Senate did not stand in the way. It is propounded as a hypothetical case, and is a pure abstraction, a nice point of political speculation, from which nothing is likely to flow but agitation, with which the country has already been too much harassed.

If we obtain from Congress all the legislation desired, and only such as is desired, and the laws should be administered in good faith by the local judges and jurors, what would we gain? Certainly no accession of political power, for the Territories have no votes in Congress or in the electoral college; and all admit that, in coming into the Union, the majority of the inhabitants can abolish slavery if they wish. If, in coming in, the majority being opposed to the institution, should be generous or forbearing enough not to abolish it, the sad spectacle would be presented of a slaveholding State sending to Congress anti-slavery Senators and Representatives. Such a state of things would certainly weaken instead of strengthening the South, and I would rather the institution should not exist at all in a State thus situated.

The South had become almost a unit on all the questions connected with slavery. Her statesmen have been striving for years to make her so. It was one of the objects dearest to that illustrious statesman of South Carolina, who, having devoted the best years of his life and the greatest powers of his exalted intellect to bringing about such unity, as the only means of preserving the Constitution and the Union, was doomed to go down to his grave when the darkest clouds were hanging over us, and our counsels were most divided. What he had failed to accomplish the continued encroachments and menacing attitude of anti-slavery fanaticism had nearly brought about, when up rises this spectre—an ideal claim—to divide us in twain. The delegates of eight States withdrew themselves from the Convention at Charleston because this dogma was not incorporated into the party creed. This movement may bring woe upon the land by the election of a Republican President. But I am not disheartened. They may retire discontented from the camp and sit moody in their tents, but those arms that have so often flashed brightly on the battle-field will hang ready on the walls, and when the hosts shall be marshaled and the loud trumpet shall sound, those eight States must be found under the sacred banner of the Constitution. We may miss them in council, but I cannot believe we will lose them in battle.

Much as I regret their course, I have no words of reproach for the seceding delegates. The motives and aims of most of them are above suspicion, and they embrace in their ranks much of the purest Jeffersonian republicanism we have in our party.

A morbid state of feeling has been engendered between the friends of prominent Democrats by constant reproaches and mutual recriminations. For months, cunning intriguers have been fanning the flame, and laborious efforts have been made by a few influential persons to plant rocks in the course of the Democratic party on which it should be wrecked, unless it should take prescribed channels. I have seen it, and have exerted my little influence in favor of concord and unity, even at the hazard of subjecting my own motives and objects to the suspicion of my most cherished friends. I hope and believe that the seceding States will return to the Convention when it reassembles at Baltimore; but whether they do or not, I have not the least doubt that their electoral votes will be cast for the nominee of the Convention when it has become apparent that either he or the nominee of the Republican party must be elected. Reproaches and vituperation are not the means by which a happier state of feeling is to be brought about.

Most, if not all the gentlemen who seceded from the Charleston Convention, declare that their constituents will secede from the Union if the Republican candidate is elected to the Presidency. I will give it as my belief that whatever may be the present purpose of the people, they will not consent to any such action, if it shall be apparent that the catastrophe has been brought upon us by the folly or division of the South. It behooves those who would band the South as one man in resistance to so deplorable a calamity, to beware how they throw obstacles in the way of our success at the ballot-box, for if the election should be lost through their errors or machinations, no power on earth can move the South to resistance.

I was reared and have spent my manhood thus far in the Democratic party. I have seen it do wrong more than once; and more than once I have seen it temporarily succumb before its adversaries. The chastisements inflicted upon it by the pleople have always been merited, and it has risen from these blows more potent than ever, because more entitled to the confidence of patriots. With these occasional exceptions it has administered the government for fifty-six years, and whilst with a steady hand it has upheld the Constitution, and maintained order throughout our extended borders, it has proved to the unbelieving statesmen and philosophers of the Old World that hostile races, diverse interests, rival religions, and apparently incompatible interests, can all coexist without collisions, and prosper under the federative republican system, administered by the Anglo-Saxon race.

Without entangling alliances or unjust wars we have absorbed almost all the nations around us, and, after teaching them how to govern themselves, have adopted them as members into the great Republic.

Without large standing armies, we have spread our people, laws, and institutions over a vast continent; watching over and protecting them in the wilderness, and, at the same time, succoring and protecting the helpless savages whom we supplant; advancing like a giant, but not crushing even the worm in our path.

Infidelity and atheism, radicalism and socialism, false philosophy and foul religions, have poured in from every part of the world. We have not attempted to exclude them, nor to crush them; but Democratic principles, like the healthful secretions of the human stomach, have corrected what was poisonous, and assimilated what was foreign, and made them all contribute to the growth and strength of the nation.

Whilst German and French statesmen and philosophers have been speculating about civilization, we have raised here on this continent political and civil institutions so perfect, and achieved results, by the application of industry and art, so grand, and established moral and social systems so pure and beautiful, that the Old World cannot exhibit a civilization surpassing our own. Annually, Europe is traversed by almost countless armed hosts, eating out the substance of the toiling masses; and decennially it is devastated by bloody wars, waged to aggrandize kings or settle their disputes. Under our wise and peaceful policy "wars and rumors of wars" rarely reach us, and the nation's might is left to slumber in the arms of freemen.

I do not deny that all this might have been accomplished under the rule of other parties; but I do say, it has not been. It has been accomplished under Democratic rule; and during all the time it has been in progress, our adversaries have been vociferating that we were ruining the country.

What party or association, in all the history of the world, save only that of the Christian Church, has contributed so much to the welfare and happiness of the human race?

Are you willing to see it broken and destroyed, so that it can never again know victory, for the sake of an abstract declaration of right, which no one pretends is of present importance? If you are not, speak out before the 18th of June. Add your voice to that of the Democracy of the Union, in urging that every district and county in the United States shall be represented at Baltimore, and in demanding that a nomination shall be made. When an aspirant has been tried, and it has been satisfactorily ascertained that he cannot be nominated according to the usages and customs of the party, let him be dropped and another tried. In this way a nomination can be made; IN THIS WAY A NOMINATION WILL BE MADE; and then a victory for the Constitution and the Union will crown our efforts.

Compared to this, how insignificant are the personal predilections that draw men together, or the animosities that sunder them! He who will thus lay his preference or his enmity on the common altar for the benefit of the country, is as much better than the intriguer or the bigot who would compel him by unfair means to do so, as patriotism is purer than selfishness.

L. O'B. BRANCH.

WASHINGTON CITY, *May* 15, 1860.

Extract from speech of L. O'B. Branch, in House of Representatives, July 24, 1856.

But it is said the bill allows the people resident there to prohibit the introduction of slavery before their admission into the Union. It contains no such feature. The 32d section declares its intent to be "to leave the people thereof perfectly free to form and regulate their domestic institutions in their own way, *subject only to the Constitution of the United States.*" If the Constitution allows them to prohibit slavery, then the bill permits it; if the Constitution does not allow them to prohibit slavery, then the bill does not permit it. The power of the people during the existence of their territorial government is a judicial question to be settled by the courts, if a case should ever arise involving the question; and whatever Congress might have said in the bill, it could not have altered the Constitution, nor taken the question out of the hands of the courts. Whatever may be the decision of the courts, I will be content; for I regard the great, main feature of the bill as infinitely transcending in importance any of the minor questions that can be raised under it. And I would rather trust the question to the people of the Territory than to such a Congress as we now have, and are liable to have at any time in the future.

Extracts from speech of L. O'B. Branch, in House of Representatives, December 18, 1856.

Mr. Speaker, when, in 1854, we accepted the Kansas and Nebraska bill, we accepted it with a perfect understanding of all its provisions. We knew that it referred the question I have been examining to the courts of the country. We aimed to refer it to that tribunal, because it was a question appropriate to the courts. We had confidence in them, and were willing to abide by their decision. We knew the act repealed the stigma upon us and our institutions which had been standing on the statute-book for more than thirty years. That commended it to our favor. But above all, we embraced it because it contained the great doctrine of non-intervention by Congress; because, under the fair and full operation of that principle, the question of slavery could no more get into Congress to furnish fuel for the fires of agitation, and to make the main element in elections; because under it we and our institutions would cease to be a football in the political arena, and because we might expect peace and security instead of the insubordination and insurrection which northern fanaticism is beginning to produce in our midst. We knew that the great evil under which we are suffering is the domestic disquiet caused by congressional agitation, and we embraced that bill cordially; not because it established slavery in the Territories, for we knew it did not, nor yet because we thought it insured the establishment of slavery; for leading southern statemen declared their great doubt whether slavery would ever be desired by the people there, and none thought the stability of the institution in the southern States depended in any degree on the decision of the people of Kansas. We embraced it because it removed an odious and unconstitutional discrimination against us, and promised to arrest congressional agitation on the subject.

* * * * * * * * * * * * * *

Mr. Speaker, I advocated the Kansas and Nebraska bill at the time it was enacted. I have advocated it throughout the long and trying ordeal through which it has passed. I stand upon the bill as it is in all its features. I will make no new issue on it, for a new issue involves renewed agitation, and a surrender of the great points already gained. Give us a faithful execution of that law, and my constituents will be satisfied. If squatter sovereignty is in it, it gets there, and can only get there by being in accordance with the Constitution of the United States; and whatever is in that instrument is right.

www.ingramcontent.com/pod-product-compliance
Lightning Source LLC
LaVergne TN
LVHW020639110826
845149LV00004B/1284
* 9 7 8 1 4 1 8 1 9 0 0 2 6 *